THI
I A
MAN
WITH

CW00371481

15:0 F.12   *M.Nl—*
                MASTER.

Regulatory Primer for
Mates & Masters

Covering Current & New Regulations
to 1 September 2011

WITHERBY Seamanship
INTERNATIONAL

Witherby Seamanship International
A Division of Witherby Publishing Group Ltd

4 Dunlop Square, Livingston, Edinburgh, EH54 8SB, Scotland, UK

Tel No: +44(0)1506 463 227 - Fax No: +44(0)1506 468 999
Email: info@emailws.com - Web: www.witherbyseamanship.com

First Published 2010
Second Edition Published 2011

Book ISBN: 978 1 85609 515 0
eBook ISBN: 978 1 85609 516 7

© Witherby Publishing Group Ltd, 2010, 2011.

British Library Cataloguing in Publication Data
A catalogue record for this book is available from the British Library.

Printed and bound by Orbital Print Ltd.

Published in 2011 by
Witherby Publishing Group Ltd
4 Dunlop Square, Livingston
Edinburgh, EH54 8SB
Scotland, UK

Tel No: +44(0)1506 463 227
Fax No: +44(0)1506 468 999

Email: info@emailws.com
www.witherbys.com

CONTENTS

Regulatory Primer for Mates & Masters
Covering Current & New Regulations

Regulatory Primer for Mates & Masters
Covering Current & New Regulations

1. Cargo Related Questions

Que. **Bulk Carrier's/Loading rates**
Loading rates on these vessels are a concern, where would you find guidance?

Ans. Recent IMO guidelines on best practice released as a circular entitled '*Additional Considerations for the Safe Loading of Bulk Carriers*' approved in May 2010.

These guidelines reinforce the existing requirements under SOLAS, Ch.VI, Reg 7.3 highlighting the risks and potential consequences of loading bulk carriers at high rates in a short period.

Note:
* The Ship's Master, who has responsibility for the safety of the ship and her crew, has the right to stop the loading of the ship at any time.
* SOLAS requires an agreed loading/unloading plan between the terminal representative and the ship.

Que. **Tankers/VOCs**
On a tanker what information would you expect to find that deals with the management of emissions of cargo vapours or VOCs (Volatile Organic Compounds) into the atmosphere.

Ans. There should be an approved VOC manual onboard that demonstrates the procedure for eliminating VOC emissions.

Que. **Tankers/VOC Management Plan**
What are the contents of a VOC Management Plan?

Ans. A vessel carrying VOC cargoes should carry and implement an administration approved VOC Management Plan which should be ship specific and at least:
- Provide written procedures for minimising VOC emissions during loading, sea passage and discharge of cargo
- give consideration to the additional VOC generated by crude oil washing
- identify a person responsible for implementing the plan.

Que. **Ports Using VECS**
You are on a tanker going to a port to load, what checks are required regarding the use of Vapour Emission Control Systems (VECS)?

Ans. The regulation applies to tankers operating in ports and terminals of signatory states which have been notified to the IMO as being designated for VOC regulation. There are 59 IMO Annex VI Signatory Nations representing 84% of the world tonnage. Operators trading to these countries will have to check whether the port is designated for VOC regulation.

Que. **Bulk Carriers/Iron Ore Fines**
What are the concerns and risks with iron ore fines cargoes?

Ans. Iron ore filings stored outside at Indian ports, which have then become saturated in the monsoon rains, were allegedly the cause of two bulker casualties in Autumn 2009. With a P&I Club working on twelve further cases involving the commodity in Autumn 2009.

The TML for iron ore fines cargoes is covered by the IMSBC code and tests have to be carried out on the cargo before it is loaded. However, if the sample is taken from close to the top of iron ore fines pile, it does not reflect the lower layer of the pile, which remains soaked even if the top has dried out.

In the hold containing cargoes of Iron ore filings where the moisture content is too high it will turns to sludge, which can result in sloshing in the holds. Once sloshing starts it is difficult to stop and often end with disastrous consequences.

Note:
Extract from Skuld P&I Club Bulletin
The most critical information is documentation stating the moisture content and the Transportable Moisture Limit (TML). A cargo is not safe for shipment when the moisture content exceeds the TML. To find out if a cargo is safe requires the Flow Moisture Point (FMP) has to be measured against which the TML is calculated.

The way these values are ascertained is by way of tests. One can do rough & ready "spot checks" with the so called "Can Test", but in order to be absolutely sure the cargo has to be tested in a lab set up specifically to deal with this issue and such test must be undertaken by suitably qualified persons. The tests have to be done for every cargo, as no two cargoes are alike.

Particular Issues
In many of the problem places, there are no good facilities to hand to undertake the tests required, with actual equipment being basic or inappropriate and requisite know-how very limited or the Code even deliberately ignored.

Cargo storage - from production to loading - may be entirely exposed to the elements and shipments may occur during high moisture/humidity/rain seasons such as the Monsoon affecting India in the Summer months.

The cargo may also be mixed in with other cargoes prior to loading, meaning it is not homogenous and while one hold's load may be perfectly safe the next hold could be a disaster waiting to happen.

Sampling and testing may at times only be done while loading is under way, the wrong cargo or parcels may be subjected to test on the shore side and indeed it is now the case that in some places the Shippers deliberately delay the provision of documentation until the last day of shipment. These quite unscrupulous people work on the basis that demand is so high for their product that they can get way with such sharp practice.

The Club has even had reports of threats of violence being made from the shore side in Mindanao, Philippines, when the ship's side wanted to question and probe the veracity of information provided and test the cargo to be loaded.

What can be done about it?
Prevention is better than the cure.

Vessels should not load if the right documentation is not provided in advance
Loading should not be undertaken if the documentation does not look sound
Loading should be stopped if there is a possible problem
Competent Surveyors with requisite local knowledge should be used every time
The extra cost and time should not be a deterrent: the consequences of a problem in terms of money and possible loss of life are simply to severe.

A Dollar saved can be many Dollars lost.

Advice to Owners
The most important starting point is to ensure that your charterparty clearly states:
Only safe cargoes may be loaded
They must always be loaded in strict conformity with the Code (and indeed any other applicable regulations and guidelines)
All necessary documentation must be provided prior to commencement of loading, and failure in this regard allows the Master to refuse loading, but with hire/laytime/demurrage continuing
Certificates must be produced by recognised reputable Testing Facilities
Require a pre-loading survey to be carried out at Charterers' time, risk and cost
The next step is to ensure the Master and the Officers are fully briefed and clued up about the problem. They must be sufficiently robust not to be fobbed off with empty promises by local Agents about the late provision of documentation or buckle under pressure from the Shore side - if in doubt the Master should contact the Clubs' Correspondent immediately for quick help and back up.

The Master should carefully examine any documentation provided - monitor the loading and raise any issues before departure with Owners, and in case of urgency with the local Correspondent. Just because it looks OK does not mean it is. The Master should do a can test.

If at any time the Master is concerned that the cargo is not safe he should call a halt to loading immediately. If on voyage the cargo liquefies and shifts the Master should immediately notify Owners, Club and seek assistance. The vessel can be minutes away from catastrophe. One Master only avoided the loss of his ship by deliberately running her aground.

Can Test
"A ship's master may carry out a check test for approximately determining the possibility of flow on board ship or at the dockside by the following auxiliary method:

Half fill a cylindrical can or similar container (0.5 to 1 litre capacity) with a sample of the material. Take the can in one hand and bring it down sharply to strike a hard surface such as a solid table from a height of about 0.2 m. Repeat the procedure 25 times at one or two second intervals. Examine the surface for free moisture or fluid conditions. If free moisture or a fluid condition appears, arrangements should be made to have additional laboratory tests conducted on the material before it is accepted for loading."

Ref: IMSBC Code (2009 Edition) Section 8 Page 33

Que. **Oil Tankers – Steam Driven Cargo Pumps**
What are the potential hazards on oil tankers with steam-driven cargo pumps that are operating in a port located in an ECA when switching from HFO to MGO?

Ans. The main safety concern is associated with switching from heavy fuel oil to marine gas oil in ships with boilers, which could increase the risk of furnace explosion caused by flame failure. The increased risk is a result of the temperature created in the boiler furnace during operation and the properties of the marine gas oil. A number of the recommended modifications when switching fuels in boilers needs to be approved by class. Therefore, oil tankers that use the boilers to operate steam-driven cargo pumps for the discharge of cargo would need to allow the boilers to cool before changing the type of fuel.

Que. **Oil Tankers – Ship-To-Ship Transfer**
There was a new chapter 8 of MARPOL on Prevention of pollution during transfer of oil cargo between oil tankers at sea that came in to force on the 1st January 2011 and will apply to oil tankers of >150 gross tonnage. What does this new chapter require?

Ans. It requires any oil tanker involved in oil cargo STS operations to carry a plan prescribing how to conduct STS operations (the STS Plan), which would be approved by its Administration. Notification to the relevant coastal State will be required not less than 48 hours in advance of the scheduled STS operations, although some relaxation to this rule is allowed in certain, very specific, cases. The regulations are not intended to apply to bunkering operations.

Que. **Cargo Carriage Rules**
What are the 'Rotterdam Rules'?

Ans. The 'Convention on Contracts for the Carriage of Goods by Sea' were adopted by the UN General Assembly, in December 2008, to "*establish a uniform and modern global legal regime governing the rights and obligations of stakeholders in the maritime transport industry under a single contract for door-to-door carriage*".

Note:
Rotterdam Rules overview:
The Rules apply to all international contracts of carriage if any one of the following is in the contracting state: place of receipt, port of loading, port of discharge or place of delivery
Charterparties are excluded.
The major selling point of the Rotterdam Rules is that e-documents will replace traditional bills of lading. Already, some IT providers, such as Electronic Shipping Solutions, are offering them.

Recap on the existing Carriage of Cargo Rules

Hague Rules and Hague-Visby Rules

The Hague and Hague-Visby Rules are the most commonly adopted rules and are used by the majority of trading countries. Under these rules, the carrier is responsible for:

Ensuring seaworthiness – at the commencement of the voyage

care of the cargo – properly load, handle stow and discharge

issuing a B/L on request of the shipper.

Hamburg Rules

These are adopted by a small number of countries, but are not generally favoured by shipowners as they allow fewer exceptions from liability for the carrier. The primary differences include:

They do not give the carrier exoneration from negligence of navigation or ship management

they govern both inward (as with Hague and Hague-Visby Rules) and outward B/L

deck cargo may only be carried if customary, under agreement and endorsed on the B/L by the carrier. Otherwise the carrier is liable for damage or loss.

Que. **Rotterdam Rules**

What is the goal of the Rotterdam rules?

Ans. The goal of the Rotterdam Rules is that:

- They are intended to provide more comprehensive rules that are better suited to modern global trade than the existing rules, which date back to the 1920s
- they include carriage of goods by container
- they should provide uniform and modernised world provisions on cargo liability
- they should provide equal status for electronic and paper documentation
- they cover multimodal carriage involving sea transportation while respecting existing unimodal conventions
- balance the interests of shipowners and shippers with regard to liability and risks.

It is intended that the Rules will ensure consistent application of commercial and legal requirements irrespective of the origin or destination of the shipped goods.

Que. **Oil Tankers – Single Hull Phase Out**

What are the phase out requirements for single hull oil tankers?

Ans. Regulation 13G of Annex I to MARPOL 73/78 came into force on 6th July 1995. It imposed requirements on existing crude oil tankers concerning double hulls, enhanced survey and scrapping, with the aim of either converting or scrapping of all single hull tankers by 2015. This Regulation is now embodied in Regulation 20 in the current consolidated edition of MARPOL.

Note:
Under the revised Regulation 13G of MARPOL Annex 1, the final phase-out dates were brought forward as follows:
Category 1 tankers (pre-MARPOL tankers) – from 2007 to 2005
Category 2 and 3 tankers (MARPOL and smaller tankers) – from 2015 to 2010.

The remaining timetable for the phasing out of single hull tankers is:

CATEGORY	DATE

Category 2:
20,000 dwt and above carrying
  • crude oil, fuel oil, heavy diesel oil or lubricating oil as cargo
30,000 dwt and above carrying
  • other oils, which do comply with the protectively located SBT requirements (MARPOL tankers)
Category 3:
5,000 dwt and above but less
  • than Category 2
	Anniversary date in 2009 for ships delivered in 1983
	
	Anniversary date in 2010 for ships delivered in 1984 or later

In the case of certain Category 2 or 3 oil tankers fitted only with double bottoms or double sides extending the entire cargo tank length and not used for the carriage of oil, and tankers fitted with double hull spaces not meeting the minimum distance protection requirements which extend to the entire cargo tank length and are not used for the carriage of oil, the Flag State may, if satisfied that the ship complies with specific conditions, permit continued operation beyond a vessel's phase-out date where the ship was in service on 1st July 2001. However, this cannot extend beyond 25 years after delivery, and these vessels will only be able to trade in a very limited area.

Que. **IMDG Code**
When does the IMDG Code, 2010 Edition come into force?

Ans. On 1st January 2012 for 2 years. However the 2010 edition can be applied voluntarily from 1st January 2011.

Que. **IMSBC Code**
Give an overview of the IMSBC Code?

Ans. On 1st January 2011, amendments to SOLAS chapter VI will enter force that make mandatory the International Maritime Solid Bulk Cargoes Code (IMSBC Code). The IMSBC Code will replace the Code of Safe Practice for Solid Bulk Cargoes (BC Code), which was first adopted as a recommendatory code in 1965 and has been updated at regular intervals since then.

The aim of the mandatory IMSBC Code is to facilitate the safe stowage and shipment of solid bulk cargoes by providing information on the dangers associated with the shipment of certain types of cargo and instructions on the appropriate procedures to be adopted.

Que. **IMSBC Code Supplement**
What is contained in the IMSBC Code Supplement?

Ans. The Supplement includes revised updates for:
- Code of Practice for the Safe Loading and Unloading of Bulk Carriers (BLU Code)
- Manual on loading and unloading of solid bulk cargoes for terminal representatives (BLU Manual)
- Uniform method of measurement of the density of bulk cargoes
- Lists of solid bulk cargoes for which a fixed gas fire-extinguishing system may be exempted or for which a fixed gas fire-extinguishing system is ineffective
- Recommendations for entering enclosed spaces aboard ships
- Recommendations on the safe use of pesticides in ships applicable to the fumigation of cargo holds
- Contact names and addresses of the offices of designated national competent authorities responsible for the safe carriage of grain and solid bulk cargoes.

Que. **Lashing Rules**
In May 2010, amendments to the Code of Safe Practice for Cargo Stowage and Securing (CSS Code) were finalised. What were these?

Ans. The purpose of these rules is to ensure that persons engaged in carrying out container securing operations on deck have safe working conditions, safe access, appropriate securing equipment and safe places of work.

The amendment is mainly required because of the high number of accidents and injuries to stevedores, who have no control over the safety standards and lashing equipment encountered onboard ships. The main design issues of concern include:
- Inadequate working platforms
- poor fall protection structures
- poor access
- insufficient working space
- difficult and awkward lashing equipment.

Instances have occurred when a ship has not been permitted to load or discharge cargo due to the unacceptable conditions onboard the vessel, leaving either the ship's crew to complete the work or the vessel to work the cargo at another, more amenable port.

Note:

IMO agreed that some sections would apply to existing ships, not just new builds, and would include maintenance, training and container design.

It was determined that reference would be made to the lashing of cargo units and vehicles on ships (Resolution (A.533 (13)) and the maximum securing load of lashings on RoRo ships (Resolution (A.581 (14)).

Lloyd's Register, along with the International Cargo Handling Coordination Association (ICHCA) and the UK Port Skills and Safety (PSS), were involved in the research. Lloyd's Register have underlined these factors in their recent Container Safe Access Report, and the findings were subsequently included in their own provisional rules. These rules cover arrangements and dimensions for access, reach limits, container securing, working spaces, STF protection, fencing and safety requirements.

A ship meeting these requirements would be eligible for Lloyd's ECL (Ergonomic Container Lashing) notation, and it has been reported that at least one container terminal will give exemption to their safety inspection vetting procedures for vessels carrying the notation.

Que.   **Offshore Vessels**

Are you aware of OVID?

Ans.   OVID is a web based inspection tool and database of inspection reports; this is underpinned with professional, trained and accredited inspectors. Released by OCIMF in early 2010, it is an aspiration that OVID will form a tool that is central to the selection and assurance of offshore vessels, complemented by an Offshore Vessel Management Self-Assessment (OVMSA) protocol, that will inform oil company assurance teams of the capabilities of the vessel/unit's managing organisation.

OVID covers the following types of offshore vessels:
- Supply vessels
- AHTS
- Standby vessels
- DSVs
- Drill ships
- Cable laying vessels
- semi-submersibles etc.

However, OVID will not include vessels such as shuttle tankers, which would already be covered in SIRE.

Note: OVID was designed to provide a number of positive benefits to OCIMF/OGP members and vessel managers. In using a database where inspection reports are available to OVID participating members, experience has demonstrated that inspection numbers will drop over time. Assurance checks as a part of the chartering process may be speeded up as the assurance personnel have access instantly to credible information on the vessel and its safety performance.

OCIMF members have cooperated to develop a common inspection document and format that will eliminate the need for inspectors to conduct inspections using a core document and client specific supplements. This should simplify the inspection process for both inspectors and ships' staff and also provide assurance personnel in the oil companies with increased confidence in the inspection report content.

The provision of a document detailing vessel/unit principal dimensions and equipment will give vessel operators the ability to 'showcase' its capabilities and provide a tool to project teams to prescreen vessels that are capable of undertaking the required activities.

Having this document controlled by the vessel/unit operator allows for rapid amendment to reflect vessel enhancements, and allow project teams to quickly evaluate the vessel's improved capabilities.

Que. **Passenger Ships – Childs Lifejackets**

What are the number of infant lifejackets that are now required to be carried on all passenger ships carrying more than 12 passengers?

Ans. All passenger ships on voyages less than 24 hours are to be provided with a number of infant lifejackets equal to at least 2.5% of the number of passengers on board.

Passenger ships on voyages of 24 hours or more are to be provided infant lifejackets for each infant on board. Also, if the adult lifejackets provided are not designed to fit persons weighing up to 140 kg and with a chest girth of up to 1,750 mm, a sufficient number of suitable accessories shall be available on board to allow them to be secured to such persons

Ref: SOLAS Ch III, Reg 7 Infant Lifejackets
Entered in to force: 01/07/2010

Que. **LSA Calculations**

If testing the SWL of LSA equipment after 01.01.2012, what must you also take in to account?

Ans. The average mass of a person, when determining the carrying capacity of survival craft is increased from 75 kg to 82.5 kg.

Note: For free-fall lifeboats, the requirements for seats, seat arrangement and passage between seats have been revised.

Que. **IBC Code**

What are the requirements for Chemical tankers during their next dry-docking after 01.01.2009?

Ans. During drydocking after 01/01/2009 before 01/01/2012
1. Bulkhead shaft glands, bearings and casings of cargo, ballast and stripping pumps driven by shafts passing through the pump room

bulkhead are to be fitted with temperature sensors (with audible and visual alarms).

2. Continuous monitoring of the pump room's atmosphere shall be provided and automatically setoff a continuous audible and visual alarm locally and in the engine control room, cargo control room and navigation bridge when the flammable vapor concentration exceeds a pre-set level which is not to be more than 10% (or 30%, for existing system) of the lower flammability limit.

3. Bilge level monitoring with alarms shall also be provided.

Que.   What is the EU ADVANCE CARGO DECLARATION REGIME / Entry Summary Declaration (ENS)?

Ans.   On the 1st January 2011, The European Union (EU) introduced a mandatory advance notification requirement regarding the import, export and transit of goods. This will be in addition to existing customs regulations. For goods being imported, cargo information in the form of an "Entry Summary Declaration" (ENS) needs to be submitted in advance to the customs office at the first port of entry into the EU. For goods being exported, cargo information is to be submitted in advance either in the form of a "Customs Declaration for Export, Re-export or Outward Processing", or if such a declaration does not apply, then in the form of an "Exit Summary Declaration" (EXS). The rules are most strict for containership operators loading outside Europe who must make the so-called Entry Summary Declaration (ENS) some 24 hours ahead of loading. For 13pp PDF go to: http://tinyurl.com/EU-Advance-cargo-Decl

2.   Regulatory Related Questions and Other Questions of Guidance

Que.   **ECAs**
What is an ECA?

Ans.   This is the abbreviation for an Emission Control Area (ECA).
An example would be the Baltic sea that was recognized as an ECA in May 2006 and the North sea in November 2007.

Que.   **Low-Sulphur Fuels and ECAs**
What are the requirements for low-sulphur fuels in NW Europe?

Ans.   Amendments to Marpol Annex VI in 2008, set a reduction of sulphur emissions in ECA's (emission control areas), these areas include the

Baltic Sea, North Sea and English Channel. Ships in these areas will need to use fuels with a sulphur content of 1.0% from July 2010 and 0.1% sulphur by 2015.

Note:
* Ships sailing in the rest of the world are working to a sulphur limit that is currently 4.5%. This will reduce to 3.5% in <insert year> and then, pending a review of low sulphur fuel availability, 0.5% in 2020.

Que. **ECAs**
Your ship is going to sail to an area that is an ECA, what must you check when planning the voyage?

Ans. That before the ship enters the ECA, that she has sufficient fuel of 1.0% sulphur content already on board.

Que. **Monitoring and Enforcing the Use of Low Sulphur Fuels in the EU**
How will authorities monitor that ships are using low sulphur fuels in the EU?

Ans. Confirmation that the sulphur content of fuel oil is within the limit is to be obtained from the bunker delivery note provision of a shipboard installation that allows a fuel oil changeover logbook entry that confirms the fuel oil changeover prior to entry into a SO_x Emission Control Area (SECA) is required port state control inspections within the scope of IMO legislation and the framework of the Paris MOU.

Control of the sulphur content of marine diesel oil used at berth (EU legislation) is performed by the Environment Ministry in co-operation with the seaport police.

Que. **Exhaust Gas Cleaning**
What are exhaust gas cleaning systems?

Ans. They are an engineering solution that provides an alternative to low sulphur fuels and can reduce sulphur emissions down to 0.1%. Removing sulphur from the engine exhaust will allow a ship to continue to use a more regular, higher sulphur content and thus cheaper marine fuel oil.

Note:
* Exhaust gas cleaning systems are reputed to cost up to $3m USD.

Que. **SO_x**
What are the chemical groupings that are commonly referred to as SO_x?

Ans. Lower sulphur oxides (S_nO, S_7O_2 and S_6O_2)
Sulphur monoxide (SO)
Sulphur dioxide (SO_2)
Sulphur trioxide (SO_3).

Que. **NO_x**
What are the chemical groupings that are commonly referred to as NO_x?

Ans. NO_x is a generic term for mono-nitrogen oxides (NO and NO_2). These oxides are produced during combustion, particularly combustion at high temperatures.

Note:
At ambient temperatures, the oxygen and nitrogen gases in air will not react with each other. In an internal combustion engine, combustion of a mixture of air and fuel produces temperatures high enough to drive endothermic reactions between atmospheric nitrogen and oxygen in the flame, yielding various oxides of nitrogen. In areas of high motor vehicle traffic, such as in large cities, the amount of nitrogen oxides emitted into the atmosphere can be quite significant.

In the presence of excess oxygen (O_2), nitric oxide (NO) will be converted to nitrogen dioxide (NO_2), with the time required dependent on the concentration in air.

Que. **Emissions – NO_x**
What are NO_x?

Ans. *NO_x is a generic term for mono-nitrogen oxides (NO and NO_2). These oxides are produced during combustion, especially combustion at high temperatures.*

At ambient temperatures, the oxygen and nitrogen gases in air will not react with each other. In an internal combustion engine, combustion of a mixture of air and fuel produces combustion temperatures high enough to drive endothermic reactions between atmospheric nitrogen and oxygen in the flame, yielding various oxides of nitrogen. In areas of high motor vehicle traffic, such as in large cities, the amount of nitrogen oxides emitted into the atmosphere can be quite significant.

In the presence of excess oxygen (O_2), nitric oxide (NO) will be converted to nitrogen dioxide (NO_2), with the time required dependent on the concentration in air.

Que. On the 1st January 2012, the EU Insurance Directive enters force for all ships. What is this?

Ans. The Directive, which member states must implement by the end of 2011, will require ships to carry on board certificates proving the existence of P&I insurance. Clubs are working towards an acceptance by states that a Certificate of Entry will be sufficient and that no special European Certificate will be required.

Que. **Ballast Water Systems – Ultimate Deadline**
By which date must ships be fitted with a ballast water treatment system?

Ans. By 2018, depending on vessel build date and class survey renewals.

Note:

The ballast water convention will come into force one year after 30 IMO member states, representing 35% of the world's tonnage, have brought the convention into national legislation.

By July 2011 it has been ratified by 28 countries representing 25.43% of world merchant shipping tonnage, with many in the industry expecting the required number to have adopted the convention by late 2011.

Que. **Do You Know the Phase-in Requirement for Ballast Water Systems on Your Last Ship?**

Ans. **Phase-in deadline for fitting installing ballast water systems**

Existing tonnage (delivered before 2009)		Newbuildings (keels laid 2009 onwards)	
Ship type	Year	Ship type	Year
Existing vessels with ballast capacity between 1,500 and 5,000 m^3	2014	Keels laid 2010 onwards, ballast capacity less than 5,000 m^3	2011
All other existing vessels (less than 1,500 cu m or higher than 5,000 m^3)	2016	Keels laid between 2009 and 2012, ballast capacity over 5,000 m^3	2016
		Keels laid 2012 onwards, ballast capacity over 5,000 m^3	Upon delivery

Note:

In state inspection terms, the deadlines are usually for the first scheduled survey after the date for the deadline.

The purchase and installation costs of a ballast water treatment plant could cost between $500,000 and $2m per vessel.

Que. Which area was designated as a special are in 2011 under Annex V of MARPOL?

Ans. 01.05.2011 was the date on which the Wider Caribbean Region was established as a Special Area.

Que. On the 1st August 2012, the 'North American Emission Control Area' is expected to come in to effect. What area does this ECA actually cover?

Ans. It comprises of the sea area located 200 nautical miles from the Atlantic, Gulf and Pacific coasts except where this impacts on the territorial waters of other States.

Que. What are the changes in sulphur limits globally after 1st January 2012?

Ans. Reduction in sulphur limit to 3.5% globally for bunker fuels. (MARPOL Annex VI - Ch 3 Reg 14)

Que. **ECDIS**
Does the fitting of ECDIS onboard mean that paper charts are now obsolete?

Ans. The International Maritime Organization rule to make ECDIS mandatory on all Solas-compliant ships by 2018 does not in itself mean paper charts need to be removed from the bridge of the ship, but if an owner installs two independent ECDIS systems that meet the requirements on a vessel they can be removed.

Que. **Fitting of ECDIS?**
What was the required date by which ECDIS would need to be fitted on your last ship?

Ans. Implementation date for ships constructed before the following dates:
- 1 July 2012 for passenger ships ≥500 gt, not later than the first survey* on or after 1 July 2014
- 1 July 2012 for tankers ≥3,000gt, not later than the first survey* on or after 1 July 2015
- 1 July 2013 for cargo ships, other than tankers, ≥50,000 gt, not later than the first survey* on or after 1 July 2016
- 1 July 2013 for cargo ships, other than tankers, ≥20,000 gt but <50,000 gt, not later than the first survey* on or after 1 July 2017
- 1 July 2013 for cargo ships, other than tankers, ≥10,000 gt but <20,000 gt, not later than the first survey* on or after 1 July 2018.

Note:
Administrations may exempt ships from implementing these requirements if they will be taken permanently out of service within two years of the specified implementation date.

* The term 'first survey' in this context means the first annual survey, the first periodical survey or the first renewal survey, whichever is due first after the date specified in the relevant regulation,

or any other survey if the Administration deems it to be reasonable and practicable, taking into account the extent of repairs and alterations being undertaken. Ref MSC.282(86)

Que.   **BNWAS**

Give an overview of a bridge navigational watch alarm system (BNWAS)?

Ans.   A BNWAS shall be in operation whenever the ship is underway at sea. Its function is to monitor bridge activity and detect operator disability, and then alert the Master or other qualified OOWs. The BNWAS will attempt to alert the on duty OOW and, if no response is achieved, will alert the Master or other OOWs.

In Operation
Once operated, the system should, within 12 minutes, initiate a visual indication on the bridge
if not reset, the BNWAS should sound a 1st stage audible alarm, on the bridge, 15 seconds after visual indication was initiated
if not reset, the BNWAS should sound a 2nd stage remote audible alarm, in the Master's and/or back-up Officers' locations, 15 seconds after the 1st stage audible alarm is initiated
if still not reset, a 3rd stage alarm should sound, at the location of further crew members capable of taking corrective action, 90 seconds after the 2nd stage alarm was initiated.

Note:
In vessels other than passenger ships, the 2nd or 3rd stage alarms may sound at the same time. In larger vessels, the delay between 2nd and 3rd stage alarms may be increased by up to 3 minutes to allow sufficient time for back-up to reach the bridge.

The reset button on the BNWAS should cancel all audible and visual alarms and initiate a further dormant period of between 3 and 12 minutes. If pressed before the expiry of a dormant period, the timer should reset.

Que.   **BNWAS**

Which ships are required to fit BNWAS (Bridge Navigational Watch Alarm Systems) by 1st July 2012?

Ans.   All passenger ships and Cargo ships $\geq$ 3,000 gt constructed before 01/07/2011.

Que.   What are the requirements for installing a bridge navigational watch alarm system (BNWAS)?

Ans.   Implementation date for ships constructed before the following dates:

- 1 July 2011 for all passenger ships, not later than the first survey* after 1 July 2012

- 1 July 2011 for cargo ships ≥3,000 gt, not later than the first survey* after 1 July 2012
- 1 July 2011 for cargo ships ≥500 gt but <3,000 gt, not later than the first survey* after 1 July 2013
- 1 July 2014 for cargo ships ≥150 gt but <500 gt, not later than the first survey* after 1 July 2014.

Note:

* The term 'first survey' in this context means the first annual survey, the first periodical survey or the first renewal survey, whichever is due first after the date specified in the relevant regulation, or any other survey if the Administration deems it to be reasonable and practicable, taking into account the extent of repairs and alterations being undertaken.

For systems installed prior to 1 July 2011, these may be exempted from full compliance with the standards adopted by the Organization, at the discretion of the Administration.

Que. **Piracy**

Where would you find information on measures and practices that you could implement onboard your ship to deter the likelihood of a Piracy attack?

Ans. There is an IMO circular on '*Piracy and armed robbery against ships in waters off the coast of Somalia*' which includes Best Management Practices to Deter Piracy in the Gulf of Aden and off the Coast of Somalia. These have been developed by industry organisations.

The Best Management Practices (BMP4) is a little blue book that was published in Summer 2011. This is a 96 page booklet that is available free of charge from chart agents and the industry trade associations.

Note:
BMP4

The purpose of the Industry Best Management Practices (BMP) is to assist ships to avoid, deter or delay piracy attacks off the coast of Somalia, including the Gulf of Aden (GoA) and the Arabian Sea area. Experience, supported by data collected by Naval forces, shows that the application of the recommendations contained within this booklet can and will make a significant difference in preventing a ship becoming a victim of piracy.

For the purposes of the BMP the term 'piracy' includes all acts of violence against ships, her crew and cargo. This includes armed robbery and attempts to board and take control of the ship, wherever this may take place.

Where possible, this booklet should be read with reference to the Maritime Security Centre – Horn of Africa website (www.mschoa.org), which provides additional and updating advice.
This BMP4 booklet updates the guidance contained within the 3rd edition of the Best Management Practice document published in August 2010.

The BMP4 booklet complements piracy guidance provided in the latest IMO MSC Circulars.

Que. **Ships Transiting Gulf of Aden**
Which route should you follow?

Ans. Merchant ships should use the Internationally Recommended Transit Corridor (IRTC) in the Gulf of Aden, in order to lessen the risk of piracy attacks. The IRTC has been established by navies operating in the region.

Ships in transit are recommended to conduct their passage through the IRTC in groups, based on planned transit speeds. The group transits are designed to ensure that ships benefit from avoiding high profile piracy areas at the most dangerous times, whilst allowing maximum coordination of military assets in the region and making ships benefit from enhanced mutual protection.

Que. **Piracy Passage Planning**
What anti piracy information is available to aid passage planning through the Red Sea?

Ans. The following guidance is provided in UKHO chart Q6099 - 'Anti Piracy Planning Chart – Red Sea, Gulf of Aden and the Arabian sea':
*   Routing guidance including the recommended transit corridor through the Gulf of Aden
*   recommended actions in the event of, or on suspicion of, piracy attacks
*   voluntary reporting requirements to UKMTO Dubai (United Kingdom Maritime Trade Operations) and MARLO (Maritime Liaison Office)
*   emergency contact details and information sources.

Que. You are to join a ship that will utilise armed security guards when transiting through the waters of the east of Africa.

Ans. In May 2011, IMO approved Interim Recommendations for Flag States regarding the use of privately contracted armed security personnel on board ships in the High Risk Area (MSC.1/Circ.1406) and Interim Guidance to shipowners, ship operators, and shipmasters on the use of privately contracted armed security personnel (PCASP) on board ships in the High Risk Area (MSC.1/Circ.1405). Both sets of guidance are aimed at addressing the complex issue of the employment of private armed security on board ships.

The guidance includes sections on risk assessment, selection criteria, insurance cover, command and control, management and use of weapons and ammunition at all times when on board and rules for the use of force as agreed between the shipowner, the private maritime security company and the Master.

Note:
Extracts from the Interim Guidance:
MSC.1/Circ.1405:
Interim Guidance to shipowners, ship operators, and shipmasters
The absence of applicable regulation and industry self regulation coupled with complex legal requirements governing the legitimate transport, carriage and use of firearms gives cause for concern. This situation is further complicated by the rapid growth in the number of Private Maritime Security Companies (PMSC) and doubts about the capabilities and maturity of some of these companies. Significant competence and quality variations are present across the spectrum of contractors offering services.

3.2 PCASP Team Size, Composition and Equipment
.3 Composition – it is important that there is an appropriate hierarchy, experience and skill mix within the onboard PCASP team. The team leader should be competent in vessel vulnerability and risk assessments and be able to advise on ship protection measures. It is recommended that one of the PCASP personnel be qualified as the team medic.
.4 Equipment requirements – this will be influenced by factors including: length of the estimated time of the vessel transit, latest threat assessment, the agreed duties of the PCASP team, (will they act as additional lookouts, utilize day and night vision equipment, assist with rigging self protection measures?) and the size and type of vessel. Enhanced medical equipment is recommended.

3.3 Command and Control of Onboard Security Team – including relationship with the Master
A shipowner/operator when entering into a contract with a PMSC should ensure that the command and control structure linking the ship operator, the Master, the ship's officers and the PCASP team leader has been clearly defined and documented.
Further, prior to boarding the PCASP, the shipowner should ensure that the Master and crew are briefed and exercises are planned and conducted so that all the roles and responsibilities are understood by all personnel on board prior to entering the High Risk Area.
.1 A clear statement that at all times the Master remains in command and retains the overriding authority on board.

3.5 Rules for the Use of Force
It is essential that all PCASP have a complete understanding of the rules for the use of force as agreed between shipowner, PMSC and Master and fully comply with them. PCASP should be fully aware that their primary function is the prevention of boarding using the minimal force necessary to do so. The PMSC should provide a detailed graduated response plan to a pirate attack as part of its teams' operational procedures.
PMSC should require their personnel to take all reasonable steps to avoid the use of force. If force is used, it should be in a manner consistent with applicable law. In no case should the use of force exceed what is strictly necessary, and in all cases should be proportionate to the threat and appropriate to the situation.
PMSC should require that their personnel not use firearms against persons except in selfdefence or defence of others against the imminent threat of death or serious injury, or to prevent the perpetration of a particularly serious crime involving grave threat to life.

3.6 Reporting and Record Keeping
The Master should maintain a log of every circumstance in which firearms are discharged, whether accidental or deliberate. Such actions should be fully documented in sufficient detail in order to produce a formal written record of the incident.

The requirements of a formal written report may be considered to include the following:
.1 Time and location of the incident;
.2 Details of events leading up to the incident;
.3 Written statements by all witnesses and those involved from the vessel crew and security team in the incident;
.4 The identity and details of personnel involved in the incident;
.5 Details of the incident;
.6 Injuries and/or material damage sustained during the incident; and
.7 Lessons learned from the incident and, where applicable, recommended procedures to prevent a recurrence of the incident.

In the event that the PCASP uses force, PCASP team leaders should be advised to photograph (if appropriate), log, report and collate contemporaneous written statements from all persons present at the incident in anticipation of legal proceedings.

In addition to incident reporting it is suggested that following a tour of duty the PCASP team should submit a full report to the shipowner / ship operator, via their employers if required, giving full details of the deployment, operational matters, any training and/or ship hardening conducted, and offering advice as to any further enhancements to security that may be considered.

MSC.1/Circ.1406
Interim Recommendations for flag States regarding the use of privately contracted armed security personnel on board ships in the High Risk Area.
Issued: 23 May 2011
http://tinyurl.com/MSC-1406

Que.   **Green Passport**
Do you know what a ships 'Green Passport' is?

Ans.   The Ship Recycling Convention introduces the concept of a ship's 'Green Passport', which is essentially an inventory of materials present in a ship's structure, systems and equipment that may be hazardous to health or the environment. This is kept up-to-date for the service life of the ship. Prior to breaking, details of any further hazards and waste material are added, which will help the recycling yard to develop a safer and more environmentally acceptable plan.

Green Passports, which are voluntary at the current time, are typically verified by Classification Societies who now provide an approval and verification service for newbuildings and existing ships.

For ISO 14001 certified companies, a Green Passport for each ship assists in demonstrating best practice in managing tonnage in an environmentally responsible manner.

Que.   **Emissions – SO_x**
What are SO_x?

Ans.   ***Sulphur oxide (SO_x) refers to one or more of the following:***
Lower sulphur oxides (S_nO, S_7O_2 and S_6O_2)

19

Sulphur monoxide (SO)
Sulphur dioxide (SO_2)
Sulphur trioxide (SO_3)

Que. **Emissions – EU ports**
What are the requirements for ships in EU member ports from 1st January 2010?

Ans. The EU directive on low sulphur fuels requires that ship's spending more than two hours either anchored or berthed in port must switch to using a marine gas oil that has a sulphur content of 0.1% or less.

Note:
Ref: Directive 2005/33/EC is intended to reduce shipping emissions of sulphur dioxide and particulates around coastal and port areas to prevent damage to the environment, human health and property, and thus reduce acid rainfall.

Que. What is Virtual Arrival?

Ans. Virtual Arrival, which is sometimes called 'eco-roueting', is the process by which a dynamic adjustment of a vessel's voyage speed is made en route to compensate for changes in the availability of a berth or ullage facilities at its destination port. The process recognises that a flexible approach to voyage times is needed due to the varying circumstances at the receiving port. For example, there may be adverse weather conditions, congestion at the berths, lack of berth space or lack of ullage space. The practice replaces the 'as fast as possible', or more recently 'as slow as possible' mantra, with 'just in time', which is a well-known and effective supply chain planning philosophy.

Que. **Goal-Based Construction Standards**
What are goal-based construction standards?

Ans. Goal-based construction standards are to be enshrined into five tiers. The standards will be set within the top three tiers and the detailed requirements in the fourth and fifth. They are not about setting standards for individual ships, but govern the development of the rules and regulations that impact on ship design.

In its very simplest form, tier one is the ultimate goal: a ship designed to have a safe operating life of 25 years. The second tier consists of the functional requirements on how that is achieved. This could consist of objectives such as sufficient structural strength, power generation, seakeeping performance, or any one of a range of other needs for the vessel to remain safe.

The third tier is the verification of compliance, by the IMO, that the detailed requirements in the final two tiers meet these stated objectives in tier two. It is currently requesting that verification documents be submitted by the end of 2012 to allow goal-based standards to be adopted and in force by 2015.

Note:
Goal Based Standards for Shipbuilding. Guidelines for Verification (non-mandatory).

Guidelines for Information to be included in a ship construction file (non mandatory) This will apply to ships:
1. building contract on or after 1 January 2015; or
2. keel lay on or after 1 January 2016; or
3. delivery on or after 1 January 2019

Que.   **The Human Element**
What do you understand by the use of the phrase 'The Human Element'?

Ans.   This is a 2010 publication sponsored by the MCA. It gives an insight as to why people take risks often with "dreadful consequences" and that decisions are a *"trade-off between: available information and available time"*.

There is a strong view that what the shipping industry really lacks is training in dealing with the human factor. This guide covers stress, the dos and don'ts of fatigue, and provides valuable advice on working with others, and communications. It also tells masters how to take control of a ship simply and effectively.

Note:
The book's inspiration was a train crash in 2002 that killed seven and injured 76. After the incident the authors wrote a 200-page guide to human factors in the rail industry. In 2008 they did a three-month feasibility study on the shipping industry. This book is the result dealing with the IMO, company boardrooms to officers and crew.

Que.   **New Rules for Hours of Rest**
What are the fitness for duty/hours of rest from STCW 2011 that enter in to force on 1st January 2011?

Ans.   • Rest periods of not less than 10 hours in any 24 hour period and 77 hours in any seven day period
• No more than two rest periods, one of which must be at least six hours; and
• Intervals of no more than 14 hours between rest periods.

Exceptions in cases of emergency and overriding operational conditions:

- Reduction in minimum rest hours to 70 in a seven day period, but for a maximum of two weeks and a gap of twice the period of exception, before there is any further exception
- Increase in rest periods from two to three — one of at least 6 hours and the others no less than one hour
- Interval between rest periods no more than 14 hours; and
- Only applicable for two days in any seven day period.

Que. What is the schedule for entry of the STCW 2011?

Ans. It is as follows:

- 1st January 2012 entry into force. Hours of Rest regulations take effect.
- 1st July 2013 approved courses have to meet and be certified in accordance with new standards. By this date governments will need to submit compliance documents to remain on 'white list'.
- 1st January 2017 full implementation, after which all standards, including certificate renewal and revalidation must be complied with.

Note:
It is intended that the regulations will be reviewed every 5 years with a full review of the Code every 10 years.

Que. The 1st January 2012 is when the revised International Convention on Standards of Training, Certification and Watchkeeping for Seafarers (the STCW Convention), and its associated Code enters force. What are the main changes to STCW?

Ans. Amongst the amendments adopted, there are a number of important changes to each chapter of the Convention and Code, including:

- Improved measures to prevent fraudulent practices associated with certificates of competency and strengthen the evaluation process (monitoring of Parties' compliance with the Convention);
- Revised requirements on hours of work and rest and new requirements for the prevention of drug and alcohol abuse, as well as updated standards relating to medical fitness standards for seafarers;
- New certification requirements for able seafarers;
- New requirements relating to training in modern technology such as electronic charts and information systems (ECDIS);
- New requirements for marine environment awareness training and training in leadership and teamwork;

- New training and certification requirements for electro-technical officers;
- Updating of competence requirements for personnel serving on board all types of tankers, including new requirements for personnel serving on liquefied gas tankers;
- New requirements for security training, as well as provisions to ensure that seafarers are properly trained to cope if their ship comes under attack by pirates;
- Introduction of modern training methodology including distance learning and web-based learning;
- New training guidance for personnel serving on board ships operating in polar waters; and
- New training guidance for personnel operating Dynamic Positioning Systems

Que. What is a stowaway?

Ans. IMO Defines a stowaway as: 'A person who is secreted on a ship, or in cargo which is subsequently loaded on the ship, without the consent of the shipowner or the Master or any other responsible person and who is detected onboard the ship after it has departed from a port, or in the cargo while unloading it in the port of arrival, and is reported as a stowaway by the Master to the appropriate authorities.'

Que. Which IMO Codes & Convention covers stowaways?

Ans.
1) The FAL Convention (Convention on the Facilitation of International Maritime Traffic) Where 2003 amendments were particularly significant to the handling of stowaways. The basic principles for dealing with stowaway situations were adopted in the 1997 Resolution A.871 (20) 'Guidelines on the Allocation of Responsibilities to Seek the Successful Resolution of Stowaway Cases' and these standards and recommendations were incorporated into the FAL Convention amendment, making them legally binding.
2) The ISPS code.

Que. Can you give an overview of LRIT?

Ans. Tracking vessels outside the range of AIS coastal networks requires satellite positioning systems. The EU LRIT satellite communication network receives information on ~9,600 EU ships' positions every 6 hours, collecting data on their identity as well as their position.

The system provides coastal States with data in sufficient time to allow the relevant government to assess the security risk posed by a ship approaching its coasts. The flag State receives 4 messages a day about the position of its ships worldwide. LRIT data is also disseminated on request to marine search and rescue centres.

The data is transmitted via satellite directly to 40 LRIT centres around the world in an ongoing exchange process.

Originally introduced to enhance security for government authorities by providing an early warning of the ships approaching their coastal waters, LRIT has also demonstrated benefits that enhance maritime safety, marine environment protection and search and rescue.

The EU LRIT Data Centre is the largest of a global network of LRIT data centres that will enable the identification and positioning of all ships over 300 Gt.

Que.   What would you find in the Ships' Routeing Guide?

Ans.   It contains all the ships' routeing measures, including mandatory ship reporting systems, adopted over the years by IMO.

Included in the publication are descriptions and definitions of the different measures adopted (in parts A and H), with individual measures outlined in detail, including reference maps and coordinates, in parts B (traffic separation schemes), C (deep-water routes), D (areas to be avoided), E (other routeing measures, such as recommended tracks, two way routes and recommended directions of traffic flow), F (the rules and recommendations on navigation that are associated with particular traffic areas and straits), G (mandatory ship reporting systems, mandatory routeing systems and mandatory no anchoring areas) and H (archipelagic sea lanes).

The latest 2010 edition includes latest amendments to existing traffic separation schemes, deep-water routes, areas to be avoided and mandatory ship reporting systems, as well as new routeing and reporting systems, including:

- In the Åland Sea and elsewhere in the Baltic Sea
- In the Mediterranean and Black Seas
- In the Red Sea
- Off the coast of Portugal.

Que.   Which areas are 'hot spots' for stowaways boarding ships?

Ans.   The hot spots include ports throughout Africa, certain South American countries and the Caribbean. Although it is difficult to predict accurately which specific ports will be a high risk at any one time, broad and relatively long-term high risk areas can be deduced from previous incidents and current events.

Que.   Who should you notify upon finding a stowaway?

Ans.   The shipowner, P&I Club and agents at the previous and next port of call should be notified as soon as possible. Local correspondents can also be contacted directly for support. Prompt contact with your P&I Club, as well as following their guidance, is the key to successfully resolving a stowaway problem. It is important that the P&I Club receives the ship's schedule and a completed stowaway questionnaire as soon as possible. This is because some ports are more agreeable to the disembarkation and repatriation of stowaways than others. The Club should also be told whether the ship is returning directly to the country of the stowaway's embarkation. One of the reasons that prompt notification is so important is that heavy fines can be imposed if ports are not informed of the presence of stowaways onboard. However, the situation can be controlled, the penalties avoided and repatriation plans drawn up if the appropriate authorities are notified.

Que.   Which ship type are stowaways most likely to target?

Ans.   Container ships. 45% stow away on the type of ship.

Container ships are particularly vulnerable to stowaway incidents for a number of reasons:

- These ships regularly trade between Europe and North America and also between African and European ports, the most desirable routes for stowaways
- empty containers present good transportation opportunities for stowaways
- container ships provide a wide variety of hiding places, with the port and starboard service tunnels being particularly at risk
- container ports are easily accessible to stowaways due to their open plan and low level of security.

Note:
General cargo ships account for less than 10% of the annual stowaway numbers.

Que.   What precautions can you take to prevent stowaways boarding while at anchor?

Ans.
- Cover and secure hawser pipes on the anchor chains
- raise gangways and accommodation ladders when not in use
- hoist the pilot ladder immediately after the pilot has left
- restrict the size of the rudder housing opening to prevent access
- retrieve rafts used for painting after completion of work
- lock deck stores
- carry out regular and frequent deck patrols with the lookout doubled in poor visibility
- make use of security lighting when available and also rig lighting to shine outboard
- be suspicious of any approaching small vessels, such as fishing or pleasure craft, as they may have intruders aboard, or even pirates. The ship should use all means available to prevent a boarding of the ship from such boats. The port authority should be informed immediately of any attempt at boarding.

Que.   Which locations onboard do stowaways tend to hide in?

Ans.   Cargo holds
- containers
- funnel casings
- chain lockers
- storerooms
- cabins
- crane cabs
- mast houses
- engine room bilges
- the rudder shaft space accessed though the rudder trunk.

Que.   **Greenhouse Gases (GHGs)**
What do you understand by the phrase: *'Common But Differential Responsibilities'*?

Ans.   The principle of Common But Differentiated Responsibility (CBDR) emerged as a principle from the 1992 Rio Earth Summit.

CBDR has two aspects. The first is the common responsibility, which arises from the concept of common heritage and common concern of humankind, and reflects the duty of States of equally sharing the burden of environmental protection for common resources; the second is the differentiated responsibility, which addresses substantive equality: unequal material, social and economic situations across States; different historical contributions to global environmental problems; and financial, technological and structural capacity to tackle those global problems. In this sense the principle establishes a conceptual framework for an equitable allocation of the costs of global environmental protection.

Que. **Port State Control**
What do you understand by the term 'Port State Control'?

Ans. Port State Control is a check on visiting foreign ships to see that they comply with international rules on safety, pollution prevention and seafarers living and working conditions. It is a means of enforcing compliance where the owner and flag State have failed in their responsibility to implement or ensure compliance. The port State can require defects to be put right, and detain the ship for this purpose if necessary. It is therefore also a port State's defence against visiting substandard shipping.

Que. On the 1st January 2011 the New Inspection Regime (NIR) of the Paris MoU on Port State entered into force. What are the key points of this New Inspection Regime (NIR)?

Ans. Key points of the NIR

- Ships will be targeted based on a risk profile that considers two elements - Ship Risk Profile and Company Performance
- the Ship Risk Profile (SRP) classifies ships into one of three categories: Low Risk Ships, Standard Risk Ships and High Risk Ships. While the SRP assesses type and age of ship, number of previous deficiencies and detentions, performance of the flag of the ship, and the performance of the recognised organisation(s), the the it also considers a Company's performance and takes into account the detention and deficiency history of all ships in a (ISM) company's fleet in the Paris MoU area in the last 36 months
- high risk ships will be due inspections every 5 - 6 months, standard risk ships every 10 - 12 months and low-risk ships every 24 - 36 months
- additional inspections may be carried out between these intervals, for reasons such as reports from pilots, collisions, groundings, etc
- the type of inspection will depend on the ship's risk profile; the minimum for a high risk ship will be an expanded inspection

- ships requiring an expanded inspection must give 72 hours notice prior to arrival.

Note:

To maintain low risk status, a vessel must have no more than 5 deficiencies during any one inspection and no detention recorded in the preceding 3 years.

Que. From 1 January 2011, under the New Inspection Regime (NIR) of the Paris MoU on Port State Control, what information must be transmitted for all ships arriving or leaving a port or anchorage within the Paris MoU region?

Ans.
- 72 hrs pre-arrival information, for any ship eligible for expanded inspection
- 24 hrs pre-arrival information for any ship bound for EU ports or anchorages
- Information regarding the ship's Actual Time of Arrival (ATA)
- Information regarding the ship's Actual Time of Departure (ATD)

Que. What is THETIS?

Ans. THETIS, which is managed by EMSA, is the new PSC information database created to support the new inspection regime of the Paris MoU. It replaces SIReNaC (Ship Inspection Report Exchange), which was used to establish white/grey/black lists. THETIS will receive information about ship calls through SafeSeaNet (SSN), which combines data received from the European Community maritime information exchange system and the Canadian and Russian Federation systems.

THETIS is:

- A new information system for PSC
- a tool for PSCOs to target ships and report inspection results
- ship call management for operational and monitoring purposes
- a database of information on ships that is connected to several other databases.

THETIS will know 'where' ships are and 'when'. With pre-arrival notification reports 72 and 24 hours before arrival, this will allow the port State to plan inspections. Every ship arriving into any port, or anchorage, within the Paris MoU region will have to provide details regarding their actual time of arrival (ATA) and departure (ATD). The reporting of this information is a requirement of the Directive and will be gathered via SafeSeaNet (SSN) and fed in to THETIS.

Que.   From 1 January 2011, what is the 'Inspection Frequency' under the New Inspection Regime (NIR) of the Paris MoU on Port State Control?

Ans.   Port State Inspections conducted under the previous regime will count. Therefore, for example, if a ship was inspected on 21st October 2010 and, under the new regime, is designated a Standard Risk ship, the window for inspection will open on 21st August 2011 (ie 10 months after last inspection) and the ship will be Priority II. The ship will become Priority I from the 21st October 2011 (ie 12 months since the last inspection) and must be inspected.

Note:

The new system is more prescriptive in that, depending on the risk profile of a ship, it will be known when the next periodic inspection is due. Therefore, for a Standard Risk ship, once an inspection has taken place the ship could expect an inspection free period of at least 10 months. The ship could be inspected within the next 2 months but will know that after 12 months it will be inspected at the next Paris MoU port.

Que.   Where would you find guidance when preparing for a Port State Control Inspection?

Ans.   A number of industry bodies (e.g. Classification Societies, P&I Clubs, etc) have produced checklists and guidance relating to preparation for PSC inspection. Companies may find these useful in ensuring that their vessels are suitably prepared for PSC inspections.

Que.   Under the New Inspection Regime (NIR) of the Paris MoU on Port State Control, what would an expanded inspection consist of?

Ans.   An expanded inspection will include a check of the overall condition, including the human element where relevant, in the following risk areas:

1. Documentation
2. Structural condition
3. Water/Weathertight condition
4. Emergency systems
5. Radio communication
6. Cargo operations including equipment
7. Fire safety
8. Alarms
9. Living and working conditions
10. Navigation equipment
11. Life saving appliances
12. Dangerous Goods

13. Propulsion and auxiliary machinery
14. Pollution prevention and, subject to their practical feasibility or any constraints relating to the safety of persons, the ship or the port, verification of the specific items in these risk areas listed for each ship type in a PSCC Instruction must be part of an expanded inspection. The inspector must use professional judgement to determine the appropriate depth of examination or testing of each specific item.

Que. Port State Control operates a policy of naming and shaming. From the 1st January 2011, substandard operators identified during PSC inspections will be 'named and shamed'. This will be via a new online register of 'name and shame' shipping companies that are performing poorly on PSC inspections, while shipowners with strong safety records will be given good public visibility. Under this regime, what is the 'White List'?

Ans. The 'White List' represents quality flags with a consistently low detention record.

Que. Who determines if a ship is to be detained after a Port State Control Inspection? how is that decision arrived at and who should the Master notify?

Ans. The Port State Control Officer (PSCO) will exercise his professional judgement in determining whether to detain the ship until the deficiencies are corrected or to allow it to sail with certain deficiencies without unreasonable danger to the safety, health, or the environment, having regard to the particular circumstances of the intended voyage.

The ship's operator should report any PSC detentions at the first opportunity to their flag state, the issuing body of the affected certificate and their ISM issuing body.

Que. Port State Control operates a policy of naming and shaming. From the 1st January 2011, substandard operators identified during PSC inspections will be 'named and shamed'. This will be via a new online register of 'name and shame' shipping companies that are performing poorly on PSC inspections, while shipowners with strong safety records will be given good public visibility. Under this regime, what is the 'Black List'?

Ans. This is a table showing the port state control performance of fleets whose detention ratio over a 3 year rolling period was above the average. The spectrum of the poor performers is ranked in 4 categories: medium risk, medium to high risk, high risk and very high risk.

Que. Your ship has been detained in port by Port State Control and the ship's operator has notified the ship's flag State, what would you expect to be the typical response from a flag State?

Ans. This will vary based on the specific flag State and the various issuing and certifying authorities concerned, but generally involves the ship's operator preparing a report of the deficiencies found, in conjunction with a root cause analysis and a note of what subsequent corrective actions have been taken to prevent reoccurrence on the company's ships.

Typically, the flag State will examine these reports and determine if any further action is appropriate. Such measures may include an additional audit of the ISM Safety Management Certificate (SMC) and/or the ISM Document of Compliance (DOC) may be required to verify that the Safety Management System is operating effectively.

If the detention occurs within the survey window for a related annual, periodical or intermediate survey, the ship can expect that this survey will require to be completed before the ship sails.

However, if the detention occurs outside of the related survey windows, the surveyor, after addressing the PSC deficiencies, will conduct a general examination of the ship, to determine if any additional surveys are required.

Depending on the flag State, further sanctions may be imposed for ships that have experienced multiple detentions in a specific period. As an example, the following is how the Bahamas Maritime Authority responds in such cases:

- If a ship has been justifiably detained twice within a period of 24 months, an immediate additional ISM SMC audit to the extent of initial audit will be required to ascertain the effectiveness of the Safety Management System on board. Furthermore, an additional ISM DOC audit to the extent of annual audit will be required not later than 30 days from the date of the detention
- if a ship has been justifiably detained three times within a period of 24 months, all statutory certificates will be suspended. In order to reinstate these, renewal surveys should be carried out with no

outstanding items or recommendations to the extent possible, and an additional ISM SMC audit to the extent of initial audit will be required. Furthermore, an additional ISM DOC audit to the extent of initial audit will be required not later than 30 days from the date of the detention

- furthermore, if a ship is justifiably detained for a fourth time within a period of 24 months, the vessel will be deleted from the Bahamas Registry. The DOC of the Manager, issued on behalf of the Administration, will be re-examined
- the imposition of a flag State Detention will have the same effect, for the purposes of this process, as a port State Detention
- the BMA will also decide the scope and extent of additional inspection or survey or additional audits of shipboard and shore based Safety Management Systems of a Company, when a significant proportion of the Company fleet is justifiably detained by PSC.

Que. Under the New Inspection Regime (NIR) of the Paris MoU on Port State Control, what does an initial inspection consist of?

Ans. An initial inspection will consist of a visit on board the ship to:

- check the certificates and documents listed in Annex 10;
- check that the overall condition and hygiene of the ship including:
  - navigation bridge
  - accommodation and galley
  - decks including forecastle
  - cargo holds/area
  - engine room

meets generally accepted international rules and standards

- verify, if it has not previously been done, whether any deficiencies found by an Authority at a previous inspection have been rectified in accordance with the time specified in the inspection report.

Que. Port State Control operates a policy of naming and shaming. From the 1st January 2011, substandard operators identified during PSC inspections will be 'named and shamed'. This will be via a new online register of 'name and shame' shipping companies that are performing poorly on PSC inspections, while shipowners with strong safety records will be given good public visibility. Under this regime, what is the 'Grey List'?

Ans. Flags with an average performance are shown on the 'Grey List'. Their appearance on this list may act as an incentive to improve and move to the 'White List'. At the same time flags at the lower end of the 'Grey List' should be careful not to neglect control over their ships and risk ending up on the 'Black List' next year.

Que. **MARPOL Amendments – Revised Annex VI**
What were the recent amendments to MARPOL Annex VI that entered in to force on 1 July 2010?

Ans. The limits applicable in Sulphur Emission Control Areas (SECAs) will be reduced to 1.00%, beginning on 1 July 2010 (from the current 1.50 %); being further reduced to 0.10 %, effective from 1 January 2015.

Note:
The revised Annex VI allows for an Emission Control Area to be designated for SO_x and particulate matter, or NO_x, or all three types of emissions from ships, subject to a proposal from a Party or Parties to the Annex, which would be considered for adoption by the Organization, if supported by a demonstrated need to prevent, reduce and control one or all three of those emissions from ships.

Que. **EPIRBS**
What requirement was introduced for all EPIRBs carried on ships from 1 July 2010?

Ans. The amendments to SOLAS Chapter IV - Radiocommunications, require ships to carry an EPIRB capable of transmitting a distress alert through the polar orbiting satellite service (COSPAS-SARSAT) operating in the 406 MHz band.

Que. **SARTS**
What regulatory changes were introduced regarding Search and Rescue Transponders (SARTs) in 2010?

Ans. From 1st January 2010 approved AIS SARTs can be carried instead of Radar SARTs. The AIS SART can be identified as a symbol depicting a circle containing a cross and the MMSI number prefix '970'.

Que. **Ballast Water Treatment Systems**
Of the many different types of new ballast water treatment systems that you will see onboard ships over the next few years, there are a number that are using Sodium Hypochlorite to treat the ballast water. Are there any concerns with this type of treatment plant?

Ans. Sodium hypochlorite is produced by the electrolysis of seawater within a hypochlorite generation cell, by the action of the seawater being forced to flow between two concentric titanium tubes that are connected to a DC (direct current) power supply.

Sodium hypochlorite solution is frequently injected into sea-chests on offshore units that are static such as oil production platforms, drilling rigs and FPSOs to combat the growth of marine organisms and algae that foul filters and seawater pipelines.

The electrolysis of seawater will produce hydrogen gas, but the quantities generated are insufficient under safe operating conditions to constitute a hazard. Hydrogen gas is extremely dangerous as it is highly flammable with its LEL 4.1% and UEL 74%.

The process of venting hydrogen from the ballast water is very important as, without the use of a hydrogen separator, it is possible for hydrogen to be introduced into the ballast water tanks where it could potentially reach a hydrogen-in-air concentration that enters the flammable range. In addition, a further hazard is that any leaks of hypochlorite mixing with acidic solutions would result in the immediate formation of chlorine (Cl_2) gas, which can be fatal.

Note:

Case Study - Operator error while hypochlorite dosing a sea-chest results in explosion

As discussed, sodium hypochlorite has been used for dosing sea-chests on offshore installations for many years and it is from that industry that we can learn further about the severity of the hazard when operating equipment that generates chlorine gas. This incident occurred on an FPSO that had been retrofitted with enlarged sea-chests to accommodate the substantial cooling needs of a petroleum processing plant.

To give an idea of the size of these sea-chests, the top mounted flange on the sea-chest was approximately 48" in diameter secured by approximately 32 bolt positions with 32-36 mm securing nuts. A change-over of the sea-chest in use, from the starboard to the port, was conducted and the starboard sea-chest duly isolated. However, the sodium hypochlorite generator was left running dosing the static volume of water in the sea-chest.

The explosion, resulting from the build-up of chlorine gas in the sea-chest some time later, tore the sea-chest flange off and bent it in with the same apparent ease as if it was the polystyrene base beneath a pizza, shearing the majority of the securing bolts in the process.

The explosion was felt all around the FPSO and she was lucky not to have suffered a worse fate after receiving an explosion to such a vulnerable area beneath her waterline.

The manufacturers comment:

We contacted all the manufacturers of ballast treatment systems that use sodium hypochlorite. They confirmed that this concern had been addressed at IMOs Marine Environmental Protection Committee and, in its simplest form, the risk could be regarded as you would the radioactive risk on an item of electronic equipment, ie yes, the risk is there but the volumes are too small. These are new technologies and new treatment methodologies that seafarers are not experienced with and the very nature of these treatment additives emphasizes the caution that they should be operated with, and never outside of the parameters determined by the manufacturer.

Que. **Amendments to ISM Code**

What were the amendments to the ISM Code that entered force on the 1st July 2010?

Ans. In addition to amending the requirements for the renewal verification and certification of the Safety Management Certificate (SMC) and the Document of Compliance (DOC), greater emphasis is placed on companies defining procedures rather than making preparations for the facilitation of them.

The changes will have an impact on the content, auditing and approval of Safety Management Systems (SMS), and in some cases may require a more detailed, prescriptive and voluminous content than presently exists.

Note:

The Company must carry out internal safety audits on board and ashore at intervals not exceeding twelve months to verify whether safety and pollution prevention activities comply with the safety management system. In exceptional circumstances, this interval may be exceeded by not more than three months.

The SMS must now be periodically reviewed by the Master. When establishing procedures for the implementation of corrective action, the procedures must now include measures intended to prevent recurrence.

Specific requirements for renewing certificates, similar to that provided for other SOLAS certificates now apply to the SMC

Que. **2010 MARPOL Annex IV Sewage Amendments**

What were the recent changes?

Ans. On 1st August 2010, the amendments to MARPOL Annex IV came in to force for existing ships.

The original legislation entered into force on 1st August 2005 applying only to new ships on international voyages of 400 gross tons and above or certified to carry more than 15 persons.

Under the regulations, ships are prohibited from discharging sewage unless one of the following criteria is complied with:

- Uncomminuted or non-disinfected sewage can only be discharged at a distance more than twelve nautical miles from the nearest land
- comminuted and disinfected sewage can be discharged at a distance more than three nautical miles from the nearest land
- certified sewage treatment plant is in operation meeting regulation 9.1.1 of Annex 5.

This requires ships to be equipped with one of the following:
- A type approved sewage treatment plant
- an approved sewage communiting and disinfecting system
- a sewage holding tank.

Que. **Ship Security Officer**
What are the requirements to perform the duties of ship security officer?

Ans. Every ship security officer shall be issued a certificate of proficiency after acquiring approved seagoing service of not less than 12 months or appropriate seagoing service and possessing knowledge of ship operations and meeting the standard of competence as set out in the STCW Code.

Que. There was a SOLAS Regulation came in to force on the 1st January 2011 concerning asbestos. What was the regulation about?

Ans. It prohibits all new installations of asbestos on board ships

Que. **Emergency Towing Arrangements – Cargo Ships >500 gt**
What are the emergency towing requirements that are coming in to force for cargo ships from 1st January 2012?

Ans. By 1st January 2012, a procedure for establishing capabilities to tow the ship from the fore and aft locations is to be provided on board all cargo ships >500 t.

This procedure is to be carried onboard for use in emergency situations and shall be based on existing arrangements and equipment available onboard the ship taking into account MSC.1/Circ.1255.

Ref: SOLAS Ch II Reg 1/3-4 Emergency Towing Procedures MSC.256(84)

Note:

Emergency towing arrangements should be designed to facilitate salvage and emergency towing operations, primarily to reduce the risk of pollution. At least one of the arrangements should, at all times, be capable of rapid deployment in the absence of main power on the ship to be towed and provide easy connection to the towing vessel.

Such fittings, located at both ends, usually consist of an anchor point in the form of a 'Smit Bracket', to which is secured a chafing chain that is led through a panama fairlead. The purpose of this arrangement is to permit a tug to take the vessel in tow in the event that the vessel starts to founder.

The principal idea is that the ship's crew, prior to abandoning the vessel, will have the opportunity to deploy the chafing chains through the panama chocks, making them accessible to arriving salvage tugs.

Even with no-one left onboard, with weather permitting, a salvage tug would then have the ability to secure a towline to the anchored chafe chain.

3.   Questions on Forthcoming Regulations Still to be Adopted

These are still to be ratified by sufficient IMO member states. Typically entering force 12 months later (check www.imo.org)

Maritime Labour Convention

The convention has been adopted by ILO (International Labour Organization) and waiting for the condition for the entry into force be met.

Once the Convention enters into force, it will require verification of seafarers' working and living condition, i.e. issues such as; payment of wages; hours of work or rest; recruitment and placement; manning levels; accommodation recreational facilities food and catering; health protection, medical care, welfare and social security protection; and seafarers' complaint procedures etc. All ships are required to be inspected but ships over 500 gt operating internationally must have certification to show the compliances. Port State Control inspections against MLC, 2006 requirements will also be carried out in addition to the inspections by the flag Administrations or organizations acting on their its behalf.

Often referred to as the seafarer's 'bill of rights' and the fourth pillar of maritime legislation after Solas, Marpol and STCW, the Convention addresses the issue of seafarers' welfare at work and sets minimum requirements for their conditions of employment, standards of accommodation, recreational facilities, food and catering, health protection, medical care, welfare and social security protection, and also sets the requirements to work on a ship.

Maritime Labour Certificate

The Maritime Labour Certificate will be a five-year certificate requiring an intermediate inspection in the second and third year. The certification process will apply to ships of 500 gt or over engaged in international voyages, flying the flag of a member state and operating from a port in another country.

Que.   MLC
What is the Maritime Labour Convention?

Ans.   A natural extension to the ILO Convention 147, Minimum Standards, encompassing and superseding the requirements of a raft of existing ILO Conventions.

Que. **MLC – Differ?**
How is MLC different from existing ILO Conventions?

Ans. It has teeth! There are requirements for regular inspection and certification, and also control by a Port State.

Que. **MLC Entry in to Force**
When do I have to comply?

Ans. We can only estimate that there will be sufficient ratifications at the end of 2010 to allow entry into force 12 months later, at the end of 2011. It may be sooner, it may be later. (check www.ILO.org)

Que. **MLC Inspections**
Who will carry out the inspection and certification for Flag?

Ans. Any Recognised Organisation (RO) will be authorised to carry out these services. The RO need not be the Classification Society for the ship, nor the ISM or ISSC provider.

Que. **Preparation for MLC Compliance**
How can a company prepare for MLC compliance?

Ans. Study the MLC requirements, in particular the Regulations and Part A of the Code. It is likely that the company already does a lot of what is required. The key steps being identifying specific procedures which need to be put into place or perhaps made more robust.

Que. **Global Sulphur Cap**
What are the changes coming in to force in 2012?

Ans. The changes to MARPOL Annex VI will see a progressive reduction in sulphur oxide (SO_x) emissions from ships, with the global sulphur cap reduced initially to 3.50% (from the current 4.50%), effective from 1 January 2012; then progressively to 0.50 %, effective from 1 January 2020, subject to a feasibility review to be completed no later than 2018.

Que. **Lifeboat Fall Preventer Devices**
What are Lifeboat fall preventer devices?

Ans. In 2009, the 86th session of IMO's Maritime Safety Committee approved Guidelines for the fitting and use of fall preventer devices (FPDs). It was emphasised that FPDs are only to be considered as an interim risk mitigation measure and are only to be used in connection with existing on-load release hooks, and that **wires or chains should not be used as FPDs** as they do not absorb shock loads.

Note:
FPDs are to be used at the discretion of the Master, pending the wide implementation of improved hook designs with enhanced safety features.

It was further recognised that a number of the current designs of on-load release hooks are designed to open under the lifeboat's own weight and often need to be held closed by the operating mechanism, with the result that any defects or faults in the operating mechanism, errors by the crew or incorrect resetting of the hook after being previously operated can result in premature release.

Ref: GUIDELINES FOR THE FITTING AND USE OF FALL PREVENTER DEVICES (FPDs) MSC.1/ Circ.1327, 11 June 2009

Que. What are the SOLAS amendments that affect lifeboat release mechanisms?

Ans. The Maritime Safety Committee of the IMO has adopted a new paragraph 5 of SOLAS regulation III/1 to require lifeboat on-load release mechanisms not complying with new International Life-Saving Appliances (LSA) Code requirements to be replaced no later than the first scheduled dry-docking of the ship after 1 July 2014 but, in any case, not later than 1 July 2019.

The SOLAS amendment, which is expected to enter into force on 1 January 2013, is intended to establish new, stricter, safety standards for lifeboat release and retrieval systems, aimed at preventing accidents during lifeboat launching, and will require the assessment and possible replacement of a large number of lifeboat release hooks.

Notes:
The 'Guidelines for evaluation and replacement of lifeboat on-load release mechanisms' ensure release mechanisms for lifeboats are replaced with those complying with new, stricter safety standards, in order to reduce the number of accidents involving lifeboats, particularly those which have occurred during drills or inspection.

New SOLAS regulation III/1.5
New SOLAS regulation III/1.5, which is expected to enter into force in mid-2012, requires that, for all ships, lifeboat on-load release mechanisms not complying with paragraphs 4.4.7.6.3 to 4.4.7.6.5 of the LSA Code, as amended by the appropriate resolution at MSC.88, shall be replaced no later than the next scheduled dry-docking of the ship. Administrations and shipowners are encouraged to evaluate existing lifeboat on-load release mechanisms in accordance with these Guidelines at the earliest available opportunity, in advance of the entry into force of SOLAS regulation III/1.5.

This is the draft text for LSA Code, paragraph 4.4.7.6.3 - 4.4.7.6.5, from MSC.87 for adoption at MSC.88

4.4.7.6.3 the mechanism shall be designed so that, when it is fully reset in the closed position, the weight of the lifeboat does not cause any force to be transmitted to the operating mechanism, which would cause any force to be transmitted to the operating mechanism, which could cause the inadvertent release of the lifeboat;

4.4.7.6.4 locking devices shall be designed so that they can not turn to open due to forces from the hook load;

4.4.7.6.5 if a hydrostatic interlock is provided, it shall automatically reset upon lifting the boat from the water.

Que. **Lifeboat Release Hooks not Meeting the Requirements**

Can you give examples of lifeboat release hooks which may not meet the relevant requirements, particularly, if they fall out of tolerance, due to wear?

Ans. Flat to flat cam hooks

Forward rotating round cam with a self-locking capability

Flat to flat cam with some self-locking capability

Que. **Lifeboat Hooks that Fail to Comply**

If a design review of lifeboat hooks reveals that a release mechanism does not comply with paragraphs 4.4.7.6.3 to 4.4.7.6.5 of the LSA Code, or a design review cannot be carried out because design documentation is not available what action should be taken?

Ans. Release mechanisms that do not comply should be replaced at the earliest available opportunity, and no later than the next scheduled dry-docking after the entry into force date.

Until the release mechanisms are replaced, additional safety measures, including use of fall prevention devices in accordance with MSC.1/Circ.1327, should be employed.

Note:

As an alternative to replacement, the hooks may be modified to comply with the requirements of paragraphs 4.4.7.6.3 to 4.4.7.6.5 of the LSA Code, as amended by the appropriate resolution at MSC.88, provided that the modifications are approved by the Administration.

Que. What do you know about the BWM Convention coming in to force?

Ans. The International Convention for the Control and Management of Ships' Ballast Water and Sediments 2004 (BWM Convention 2004) will come in to force 12 months after ratification by 30 States, representing 35 per cent of world merchant shipping tonnage.

(July 2011 it has been ratified by 28 countries representing 25.43% of world merchant shipping tonnage).

Que. **Asbestos**

What wert the regulatory changes to SOLAS that were introduced on 1st January 2011 concerning asbestos?

Ans. The new installation of materials containing asbestos will be prohibited on all ships.

Ref: SOLAS Ch II-1, Reg 3-5